D1066920

A Baby Is...

A Baby Is...

A book of the triumphs, tribulations and tender times with infants

by Karol Cooper

WALNUT GROVE PRESS
Nashville, TN 37211

ISBN 1-58334-098-X

Material for this book was obtained mostly from secondary sources, primarily print media. While every effort was made to ensure the accuracy of these sources, the accuracy cannot be guaranteed. For additions, deletions, corrections or clarifications in future editions of this text, please write Walnut Grove Press.

Printed in the United States of America
Cover Design & Page Layout: *Bart Dawson*
Typesetting & Page Layout: *Karol Cooper*

1 2 3 4 5 6 7 8 9 10 • 01 02 03 04 05 06 07 08 09 10

Special Thanks to Lisa, Wanda, Miss B, and Lisha, who took the time from their busy schedules to answer my baby questions; to Criswell for being such a great guy; and to all the staff at WGP.

for my sister Kathy
who loves babies,
and for my sister Karla
who loves cats

and as always, for Alan.

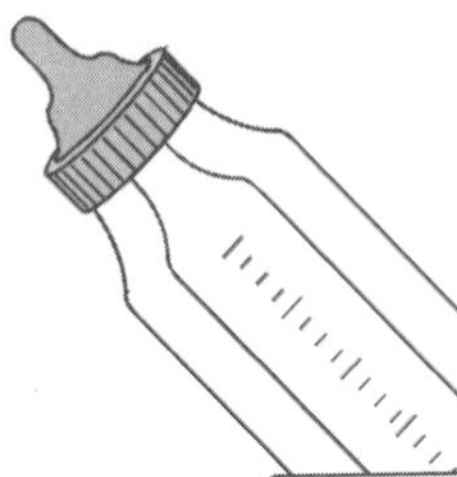

Table of Contents

I don't know nuthin
'bout birthin no babies!

Prissy
Gone With the Wind

A Baby Is...

When the first baby laughed for the first time, the laugh broke into a thousand pieces and they all went skipping about, and that was the beginning of fairies. And now when every new baby is born its first laugh becomes a fairy.

James Matthew Barrie

Chapter 1

A Baby Is...

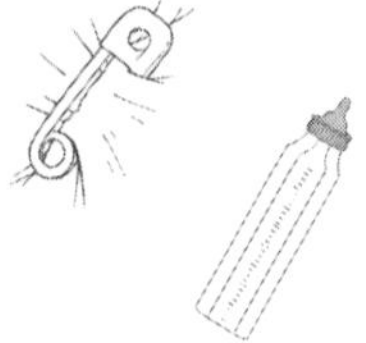

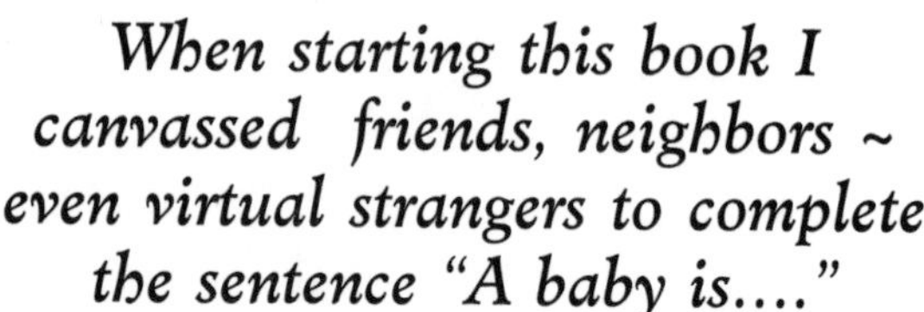

When starting this book I canvassed friends, neighbors ~ even virtual strangers to complete the sentence "A baby is...."

From six-year-old girls to doting grandfathers, from new parents to great-grandparents, from neighbors to the mailman to the road crew, the response was universal:

~

a baby is to love.

Nothing triggers our protective urges, softens our hearts, captures our imaginations, or inspires such awe as a tiny, helpless infant.

kc

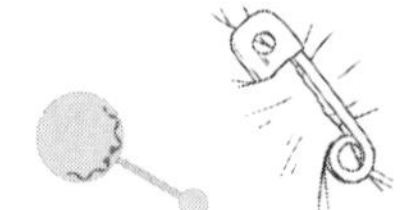

A baby is...

~

love and laughter and tears and joy and frustration all wrapped up in a tiny bundle.

~

better than TV. Ever watch a group of adults when a baby is in the room?

~

a chance to look at the world again ~ to begin fresh and see everything in all its wonder all over again, to marvel at an ant crawling or a butterfly fluttering by or an airplane flying over.

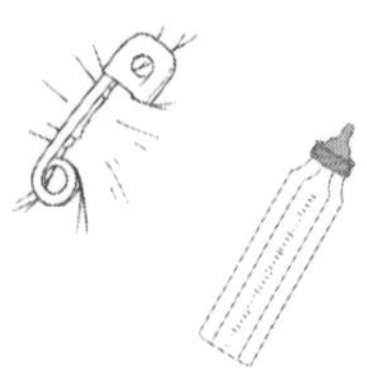

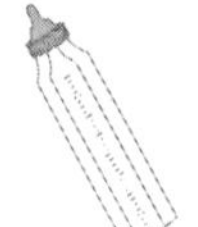

A baby is...

~

a most treasured toothless wonder.

~

the most important job you'll ever have.

~

a daily reminder of selfless giving and loving.

~

the ultimate expression of love.

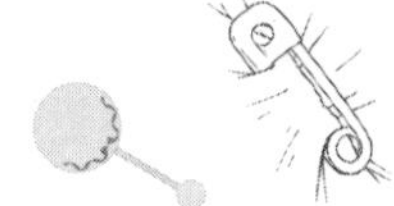

A baby is...

~

the most all-encompassing, totally mysterious, life-altering, challenging, completely fantastic little bundle of the most love and joy imaginable.

~

the best gift from Heaven.

~

the reason for breathing.

~

the person we sacrifice anything for and it feels like absolutely no big deal.

~

our teacher, our tears,
our warmest embrace.

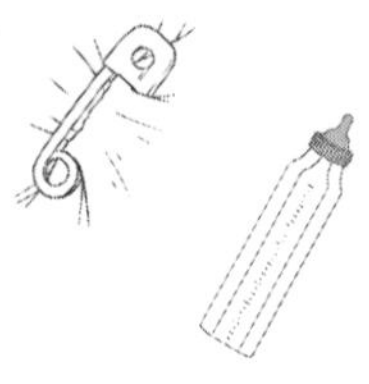

A baby is
a kiss factory.
No matter how many kisses
you steal, they still have an
abundant supply.

Kathy Prince

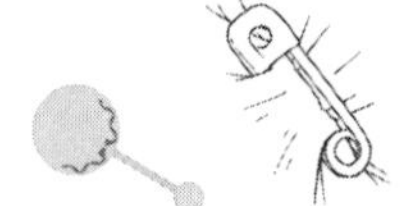

A baby is...

~

light in the midst of darkness.

~

joy beyond measure.

~

a voice that opens eyes.

~

the completion of your heart.

~

a clean canvas in need of painting.

~

shining glory, sleepless nights, deepest worry, endless love.

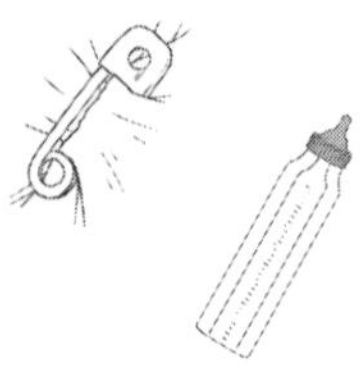

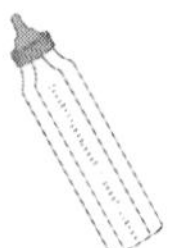

A baby is...

~

bits of stardust
blown from the hand of God.

~

such a nice way to start people.

~

a work of art created by God for his pleasure.

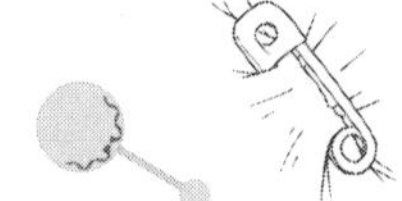

A baby is
an angel whose wings decrease as his
legs increase.

May Sarton

~

A baby is
still the symbol of
the eternal marriage
between love and duty.

George Eliot Romola

~

A baby is
God's opinion
that the world should go on.

Carl Sandburg

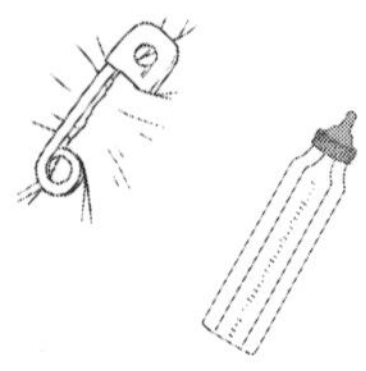

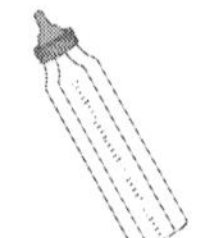

A baby is
the beginning of all things:
wonder, hope, a dream of
possibilities. In a world that is
cutting down its trees to build
highways, babies are almost the
only remaining link with nature
from which we spring.

Eda LeShan

~

A baby is
an inestimable blessing.

Mark Twain

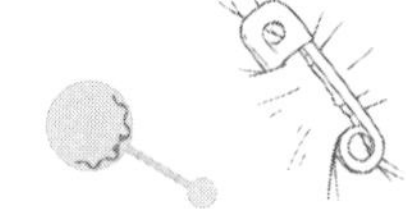

A baby is
on loan from God.

Wanda Woodard

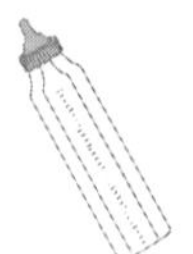

A baby is...

~

your own personal alarm clock!

~

a teeny tiny bundle
of teeny tiny toes
and teeny tiny fingers
and teeny tiny eyelashes
and teeny tiny ears ~
all more precious than jewels.

~

our own little angel.

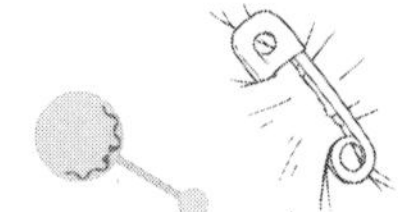

A baby is hope.

Caroline Foxx

To see a newborn is
to be humbled,
to forget our own egos,
to realize how little we do to
affect the mystery of creation.

Mike Samuels, M.D.
Nancy Samuels

Chapter 2

The Thrill of It All

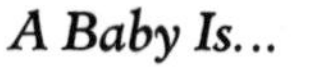
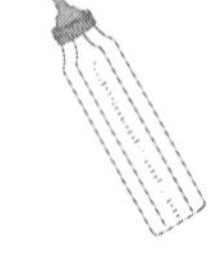

Even newborns
get lint between their toes.

Amy Krouse Rosenthal

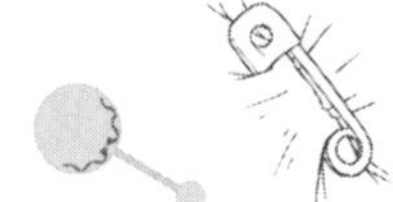

Father asked us what was
God's noblest work.
I said babies.

Louisa May Alcott

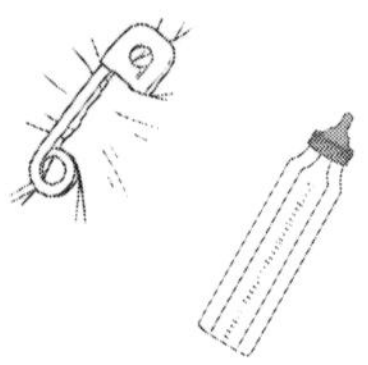

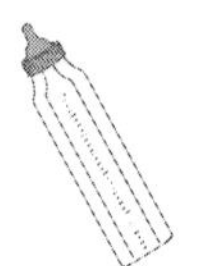

Every child
is born a genius.

R. Buckminster Fuller

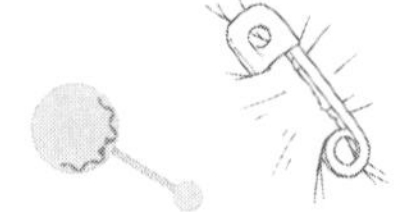

I want her to grow up feeling totally
and unconditionally loved.

Jacqueline Frost

The newborn has an incredible radiance
which evokes universal awe and love.

Mike Samuels, M.D.
Nancy Samuels

Flowers are words
which even a baby can understand.

Arthur C. Coxe

Children are the only form of
immortality that we can be sure of.

Peter Ustinov

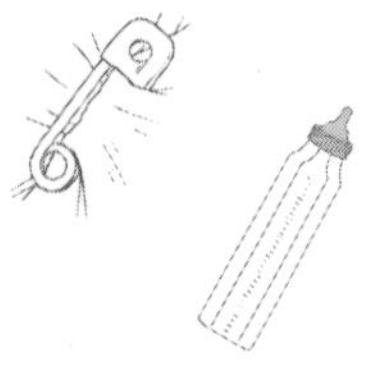

Trust yourself.
You know more
than you think you do.

Dr. Benjamin Spock

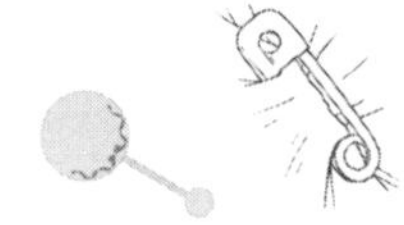

We have children because
we want immortality,
and this is the most reliable
way of getting it.

Woodrow Wyatt

At every step the child
should be allowed to meet
the real experience of life;
the thorns should never
be plucked from its rose.

Nora Ephrom

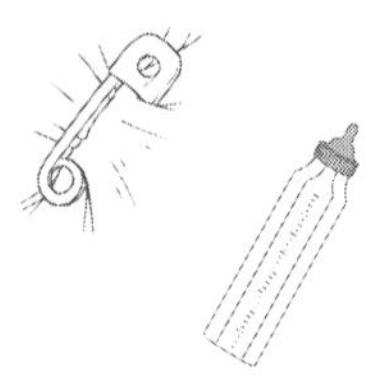

When babies stare
at objects around them,
they are actually learning to
organize their experience.
By observing similarities and
slight differences, babies form
basic concepts.

Mike Samuels, M.D.
Nancy Samuels

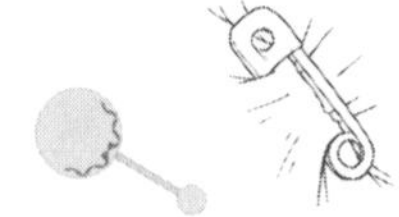

With each child
the world begins anew.

Midrash

The soul is healed
by being with children.

Fyodor Dostoyevsky

Children are a poor man's riches.

English proverb

Children are the hands
by which we take hold of heaven.

Henry Ward Beecher

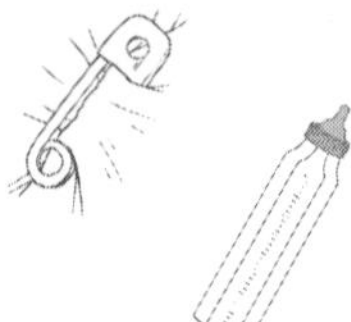

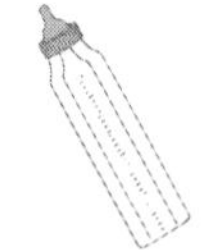

Children are like snowflakes,
unique, fragile and fleeting.

Stefanie Thomas

While all babies are naturally endowed
with fantastic capabilities,
each baby is unique in the way
it responds to the world.
From birth each baby is an individual.
And each mother is unique.
Thus every mother-child interaction will
be a special one ~ broadly like others,
but distinct in many respects.

Mike Samuels, M.D.
Nancy Samuels

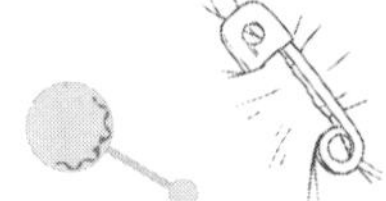

In automobile terms,
the child supplies the power
but the parents have to do
the steering.

Dr. Benjamin Spock

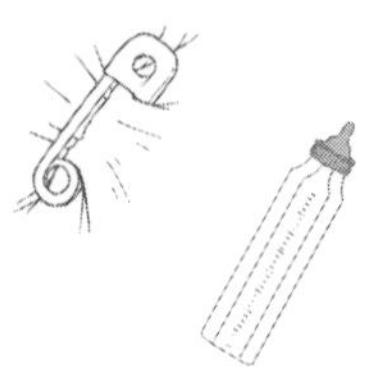

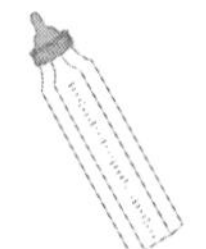

When you were born,
you cried,
and the world rejoiced.

Native American saying

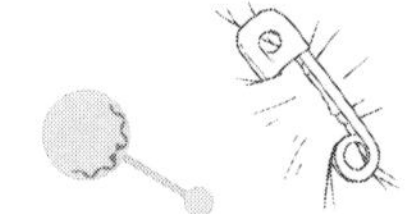

The baby gets the gift of
the parents' whole lives.

Mike Samuels, M.D.
Nancy Samuels

A mother's children are
portraits of herself.

Anonymous

We find delight in the beauty and
happiness of children that makes
the heart too big for the body.

Ralph Waldo Emerson

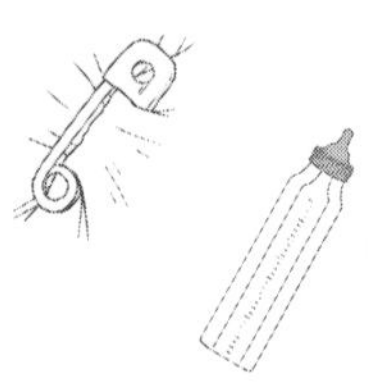

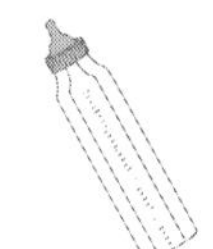

In a rich, full relationship
between mother and baby,
the mother naturally stimulates
the baby through her attention
and encouragement.

Mike Samuels, M.D.
Nancy Samuels

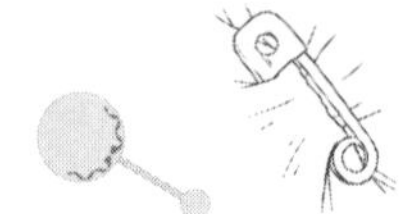

Children need love, especially when they do not deserve it.

Harold Hulbert

Children have never been very good at listening to their elders, but they have never failed to imitate them.

James Baldwin

I used to be a worrier...
when the children were babies, I used to get up at night and hold a mirror under their nostrils to make sure they were still breathing.

Erma Bombeck

You were our first miracle. You were the genesis of a marriage, the fulfillment of young love, the promise of our infinity. You were new, had unused grandparents, and had more clothes than a Barbie doll. You were the "original model" for unsure parents trying to work the bugs out. You got the strained lamb, open pins and three-hour naps. You were the beginning.

Erma Bombeck

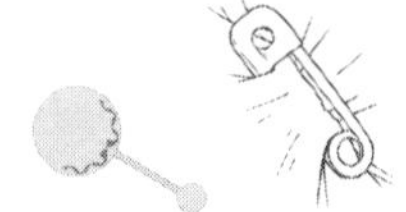

Childbirth is, by nature, miraculous ~
regardless of how many or how few
people you have with you.
But it seems auspicious for a child to
enter a place filled with love and
rejoicing, a friendly warm environment
for the new little person.

Gopi

There's nothing in the world more
fascinating than watching a child grow
and develop. At first you think of it as
just a matter of growing bigger. Then, as
the infant begins to do things, you may
think of it as "learning tricks." But it's
really more complicated and full of
meaning than that. The development of
each child retraces the whole history of
the human race, physically and spiritually,
step by step.

Dr. Benjamin Spock

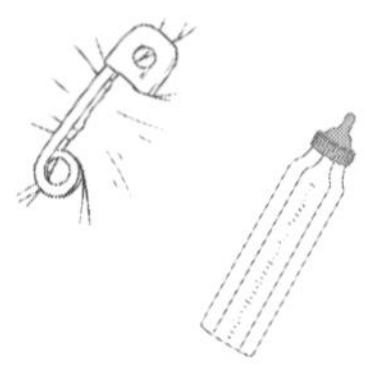

Mothering is really a continuance of the closeness of the prenatal state, and the more clearly it imitates certain of the conditions before birth the more successful it is in the first weeks.

Margaret A. Ribble, MD

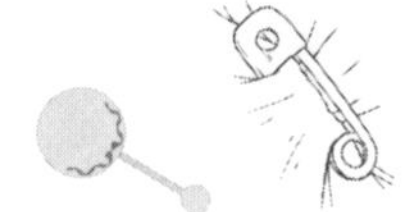

Infant Joy

I have no name
I am but two days old.
What shall I call thee?
"I happy am,
Joy is my name."
Sweet joy befall thee!

Pretty joy!
Sweet joy, but two days old
Sweet joy I call thee:
Thou dost smile,
I sing the while;
Sweet joy befall thee!

William Blake
Songs of Innocence

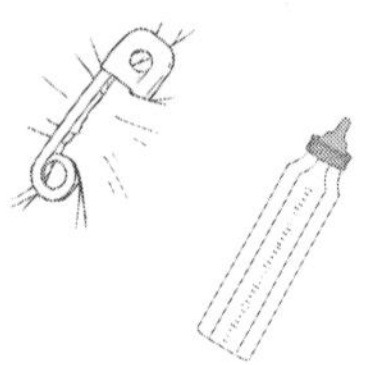

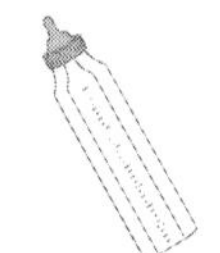

I never understood why babies were created with all the component parts necessary for a rich, full life...with the unfinished plumbing left to amateurs.

Erma Bombeck

The parent hovers over the baby ~ alternately worrying and giving encouragement as the baby is about to take its first steps.

The Well Baby Book

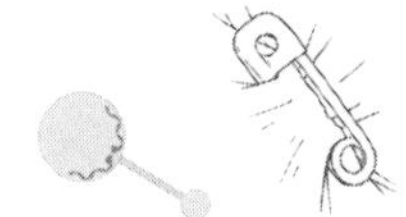

The end product of a family's training is always a precise picture of the family's character.

Carlyle Marney

We can more easily communicate with our babies if we try our best to see things from their viewpoint.

Joan Wiener
Joyce Glick

It is easier to build strong children than to repair broken adults.

Frederick Douglas

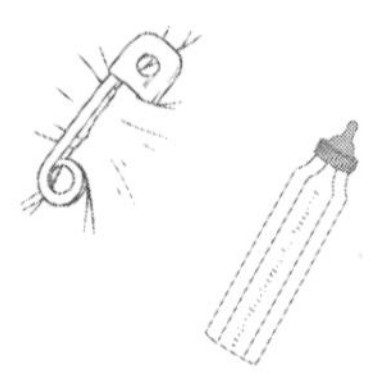

Babies have a right to develop to the fullest the natural resources of life energy within them called instinct. This is the motive power not only for physical activity but also for mental function. Like all the other primary forces of nature this energy must have guidance and direction from the beginning.

Margaret A. Ribble, MD

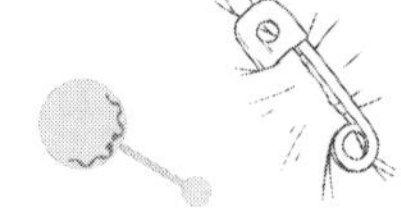

The Commandments of Parents

- Thou shalt not be inconsistent in order to keep him close.

- Thou shalt not threaten in order to gain thy way.

- Thou shalt not transfer thine own neurotic fears in order to control him.

- Thou shalt not break promises in order to subdue him.

- Thou shalt not bribe him to do what is right.

- Thou shalt neither lie to him nor for him.

- Nor shalt thou shield him in any other way from the consequences of his own acts.

Carlyle Marney

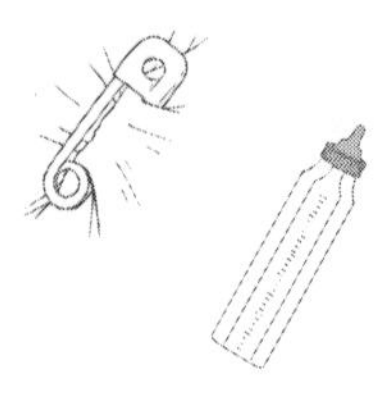

The newborn's hands
and feet are always
a source of amazement
because they are so perfectly
and minutely formed.

The Well Baby Book

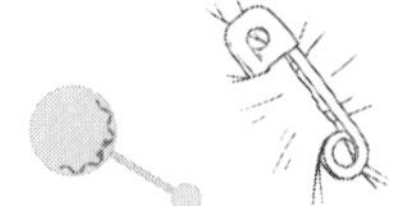

The baby is never a
silent partner in the first
relationship with his mother.
He both propels himself and is
propelled into a world which is
completely unfamiliar.

Margaret A. Ribble, MD

One of the great things about our culture is the accessibility of information for new parents. One of the best sources of that information is our friends. Relying on the advice and feedback of friends and family supplies us with generations of child-rearing knowledge and experience. Don't be afraid to ask for advice! You don't have to take it. But listening to the voice of experienced parents makes the job of child rearing more manageable.

Caroline Foxx

Chapter 3

A Little Help From My Friends

How to fold a diaper
depends on the size of the baby
and the diaper.

Dr. Benjamin Spock

Diapers

Back in the olden days when my kids were babies, diapering took on a whole new aspect. As an avid new mother I refused to let paper diapers touch my first baby's bottom ~ an insane condition that was soon remedied by the births of subsequent children.

How times have changed!
Now we have so many choices ~ diapers in every conceivable size, with decorations, elastic legs, pull-ups, just for girls, just for boys...

Following are a few tips from veteran moms...

- Don't buy cheap disposable diapers. Save money in other ways ~ the cheap ones just don't cut it. They leak, baby is miserable, ma-ma exhausted.

- Have one of your showers (moms-to-be) just for supplies, especially diapers. YOU CANNOT HAVE ENOUGH DIAPERS!

- Stockpile diapers! Or else it's like a car payment every month to buy a supply.

- Diapering can be a playtime for the newborn, who spends much of his time asleep.

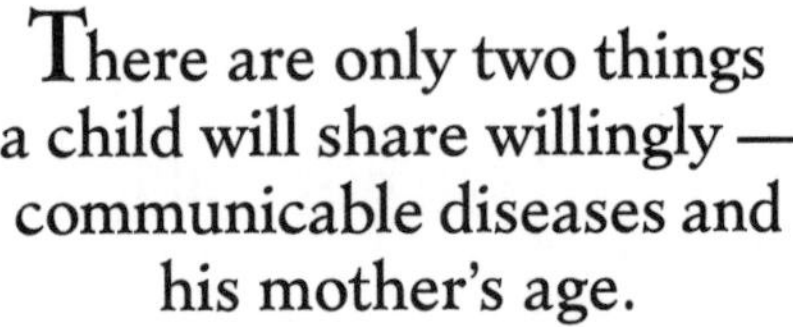

There are only two things
a child will share willingly —
communicable diseases and
his mother's age.

Dr. Benjamin Spock

Sick Baby

Almost all of us remember special treatment from our mothers during our childhood illnesses. Mama's loving care (or Dad's) was the basis of our healing, and even today when we hit rock bottom, we want our Mama / we want our Daddy! Here are some favorite sickbed remedies:

- Cream cheese on bagels
- Chicken soup and ginger ale
- A spot of perfume on the wrist
- A flower beside the bed
- Anything on a tray

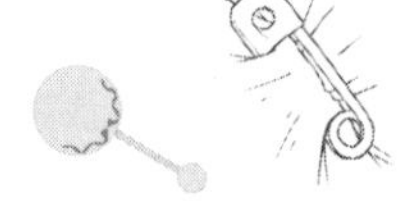

Buy the super-expensive ear thermometer, or better yet let a do-good family member get it. The rectal thermometer is, well, rectal. Need I say more? When it's three o'clock in the morning and you think they're dying...sticking it in the ear is easier.

Lisa Holifield

Soothing Techniques

Feed the Baby
Burp the baby
Change diaper
Pick up on shoulder and hold
Rock the baby
Walk the baby
Pat the baby while it lies on stomach
Talk to baby
Put baby where it can see action
Distract the baby
Give baby a pacifier
Play quiet serene music

The Well Baby Book

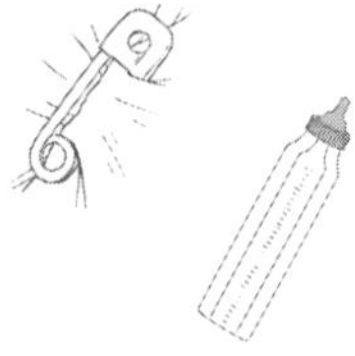

Colic

Colic is a poorly defined condition in which an otherwise healthy baby cries excessively. Some pediatricians classify as colicky those babies who have crying fits more than three hours a day, three days a week. Often these babies draw up their knees and have obvious gas, causing parents to report that the babies have abdominal discomfort. But no studies indicate any abdominal problem or that these babies are fundamentally different from other babies.

The Well Baby Book

~

If you never had a colicky baby, thank your lucky stars. Nothing can make us feel more helpless than a beet-red, screaming baby. Nothing seems to work, the baby screams endlessly, mom and dad's nerves are fried. What's a parent to do?

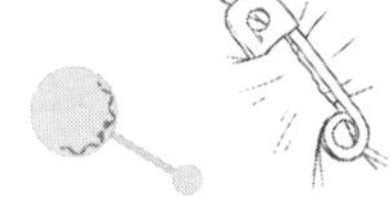

After weeks of baby's screaming with colic, I decided enough was enough. I made the decision to try the old country cure for colic: a tablespoon of whiskey, a tablespoon of honey, a squirt of lemon, heated and down the hatch. Since we were not drinkers, and I didn't want to invest in a full bottle of whiskey, I stopped at a local bar and asked for a little bit of whiskey "to go." The bartender, remembering the horrors of colic, took mercy on me and gave me a few shots in a little paper cup to take home. I don't remember if it cured the baby's colic, but the shots I drank sure helped.

Nevin Allingham

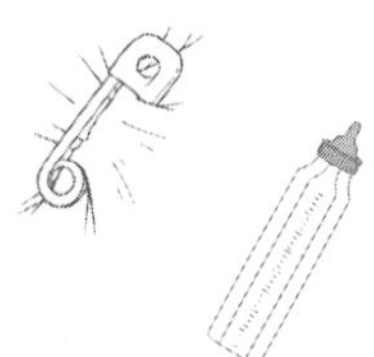

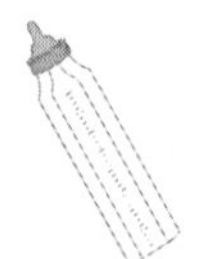

The most important thing is for the mother and father to recognize that the condition known as colic is fairly common, that it doesn't seem to do the baby any permanent harm, that on the contrary, it occurs most often in babies who are developing and growing well, and that it will probably be gone by the time the baby is three months old.

Dr. Benjamin Spock

The only way our baby would sleep was in her car seat on top of the clothes dryer. The combo of heat and motion finally helped her sleep. We were so scared of it that we got bungee cords to tie it to the machine.

Lisa Holifield

My first baby's pediatrician was a life-saver. He explained that in "primitive" cultures colic is never a problem. Primitive mothers, understanding that their infants had spent all of their prenatal lives close to Mom, strapped the baby across their chests and went back to work in the fields. Keep your baby close to your heart. The natural sounds and rhythms of your body comfort your baby.

Caroline Foxx

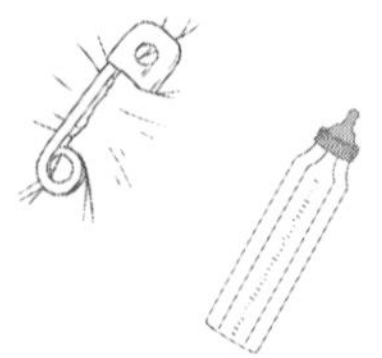

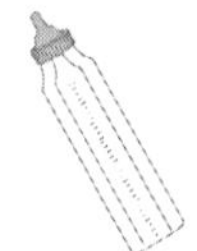

If you put a baseball and other
toys in front of a baby,
he'll pick up the baseball in
preference to the others.

Tris Speaker
Baseball Hall of Famer

Play

Play is important for baby. It's important for parents to have fun with the baby. It's also important for parents to have fun together without *the baby! Don't forget playtime for Mom and Dad!*

He's getting a sense of how much you mean to each other. When you hug him or make noises at him, when you show him that you think he's the most wonderful baby in the world, it makes his spirit grow, just like milk makes his bones grow.

Dr. Benjamin Spock

At some point you'll probaby be confronted with a choice between your material possessions and your child's inquisitive nature.

Joan Wiener
Joyce Glick

Most normal babies respond well to a certain amount of jiggling.

Margaret A. Ribble, MD

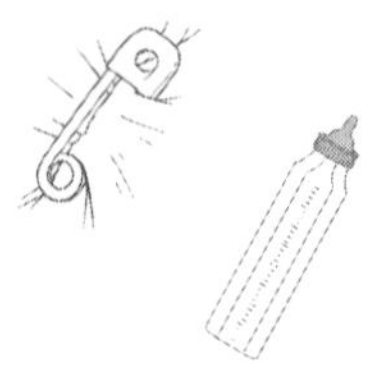

I developed a "thing" about germs. When I changed diapers, I washed *their* hands.

Erma Bombeck

Laundry

Laundry? ***Expect a lot of it.***
Little babies use a lot of little clothes, and having little babies makes us use a lot of clothes for ourselves. There are some days when that pile of laundry may look like Pike's Peak. During the early years with my boys, our home movies showed them playing, and me doing laundry; them laughing, and me doing laundry; them tucked in asleep like angels, and me ~ you guessed it ~ still doing laundry.

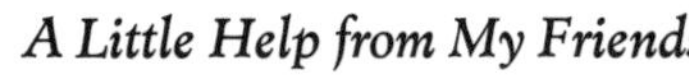

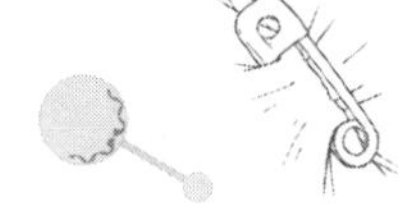

- Get a large pad for the bed so that when the diapers leak at night (and they will), you are not changing sheets and padding every day.

- Get a little mesh bag to wash their tiny socks in, or they will forever be lost in sock heaven somewhere in the washer.

- If baby doesn't have sensitive skin, forget that snow detergent...very pricey and not so effective, and you lose your mind trying to wash all their stuff separately.

Lisa Holifield

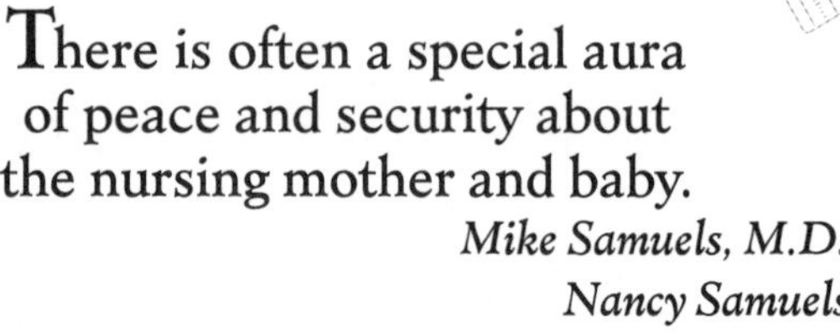

There is often a special aura of peace and security about the nursing mother and baby.

Mike Samuels, M.D.
Nancy Samuels

Feeding

Breast-feeding can be one of the most rewarding, life enhancing experiences of bonding that a mother will know in her lifetime with a child. It can also be a pain in the behind. I nursed all three of my sons, and I remember well the first months of discomfort, the learning, the wet spots on my shirts. Without the invaluable advice and support of La Leche League I wouldn't have been successful. Please, please contact them if you are nursing or planning to nurse your baby. Whether you breast-feed or bottle-feed, mealtimes are a source of real joy and intimate exchange between parent and baby.

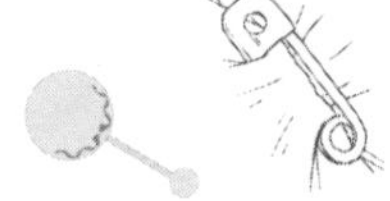

The playtex nurser kit... I thought I'd lose my mind trying to breast-feed, and this kit is a life-saver. Seems more mom-like and my baby took to it instantly.

Lisa Holifield

I nursed all my kids and was blessed with abundant supply. So I expressed the leftovers into Playtex Nurser bags and froze them. When I had to be away from baby, I simply defrosted a couple of bags.

Sheila Stone

The age of weaning is highly variable in our culture. In the second half of the first year, the baby can still enjoy the physical and social benefits of breast-feeding. Gradual weaning allows the baby to master a new skill without too much pressure.

The Well Baby Book

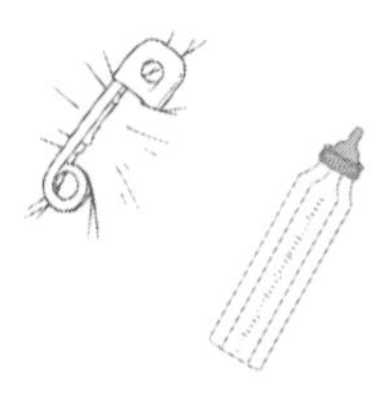

By the end of the first year, babies show great attachment to their mothers. This attachment is demonstrated by loving gestures as well as by staying physically close to the mother.

The Well Baby Book

For success in training
children the first condition is
to become as a child oneself,
but this means
no assumed childishness,
no condescending baby-talk ...
What it does mean is to be
taken up with the child as
the child himself is absorbed
by his life.

Ellen Key

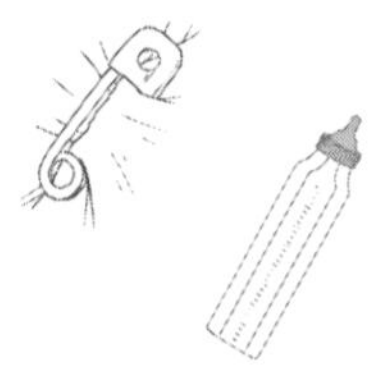

During the last decade we have learned that infants only hours old have acute pattern vision. At a distance of ten inches, infants can resolve or focus on eight-inch stripes. Infants fix their gaze on specific targets and deliberately choose to look at patterns rather than solid colors, and look at facelike patterns rather than others. This visual ability immediately fosters interaction with the mother, which in turn gives her pleasure and stimulates her maternal feelings.

The Well Baby Book

Except that right side up is best, there is not much to learn about holding a baby. There are 152 distinctly different ways — and all are right!

Heywood C. Broun

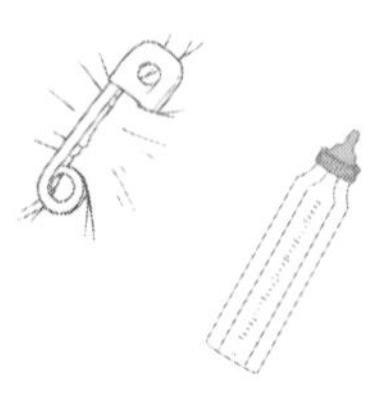

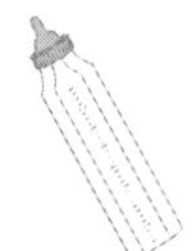

Take advantage of the baby's naps to relax yourself deeply.

~

The spiritual bond between mother and baby deepens as the baby grows. The baby comes to realize that the mother is the source of its sustenance, and the mother in turn begins to have a sense of the baby's unfolding personality.

Mike Samuels, M.D.
Nancy Samuels

Take several deep breaths if you are frightened, frustrated, or angered by the baby.

~

Who is this being? The change in our relationship from a tight unit to two people is causing culture shock. It seemed I knew her so much better before I ever saw her, when it was all feeling, all spirit.

Kathy Humphrey

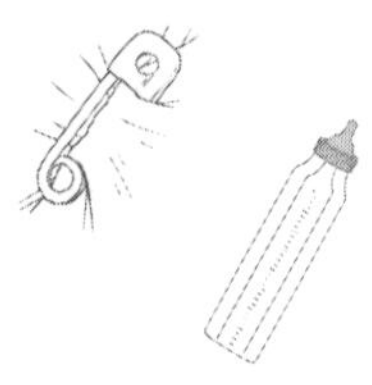

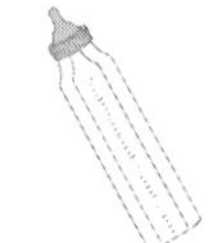

The more people have studied different methods of bringing up children the more they have come to the conclusion that what good mothers and fathers instinctively feel like doing for their babies is the best after all.

Dr. Benjamin Spock

A baby is born with
a need to be loved and
never outgrows it.

Frank A. Clarke

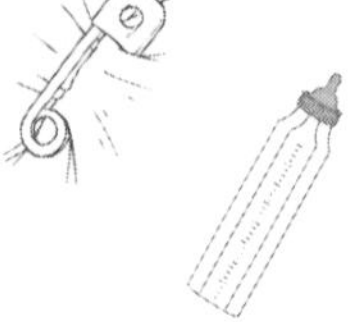

We cannot experiment on human babies and give them the prescribed amount of positive and negative emotions, but we are able to observe the experiments which Nature makes.

Margaret A. Ribble, MD

Afraid of the Dark

A first fear of the infant is fear of the dark. Darkness separates him from his mother. This illustrates well the relationship between internal and external fear. It seems to be due to two factors: it shuts him off from the mother, whom he cannot see,and also deprives him of a still more primitive satisfaction, one that comes from the stimulation of light.

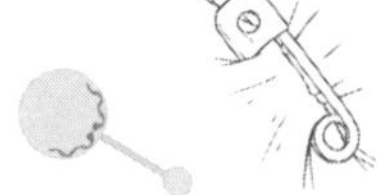

One of the best stories I've heard about dealing with night fears is from my son, Ben. When he was about four years old, we were gathered with his dad's rather large family in one of the sibling's houses. The 12 kids had been put to bed in various and sundry corners of the house. But Ben simply couldn't sleep ~ he was too scared of monsters in the room. His dad and I tried every soothing trick up our sleeves, but he simply couldn't settle down. Enter Uncle Nevin, who slammed open the door to the bedroom, burst into the room in a ninja crouch, and then proceeded to fight and wrestle all of the "monsters" in the room. For at least a full five minutes we listened from downstairs to the bumps and bangs from the upstairs bedroom. When Uncle Nevin was done, all monsters had been banished and Ben was asleep. But he remembers to this day how important it was to have someone take his fears "seriously."

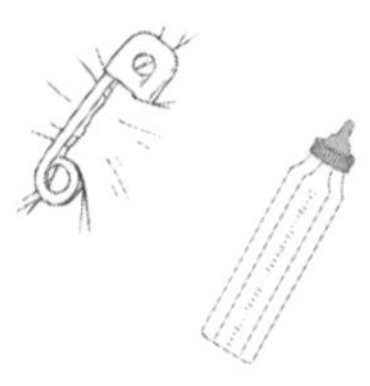

With consignment shopping for baby clothes, like-new clothing can be purchased for far, far less; and the way babies grow, their clothes wear out in short time, and before you know it, they've grown out of them. Worth an investment: shoes. Bad shoes, worn-out looking baby!

Lisa Holifield

One of the most wonderful ways that we "get a little help from our friends" with our newborns is through the sharing of baby clothes and furnishings. During my child-bearing years I was fortunate to have a group of women friends with whom to share. This system allowed us to purchase those "special occasion" clothes that are so adorable ~ and so expensive.

Diana Clark

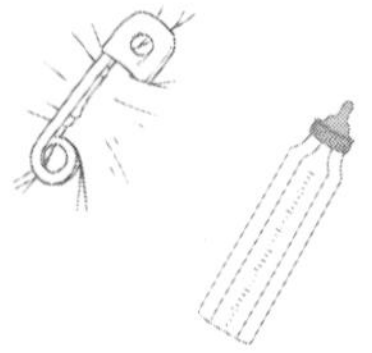

Diaper rash?
If you're using disposable
diapers, switch to another brand.
Often perfumes or dyes can be
the culprit. I found that the cheaper
the diaper, the nastier the rash.

Caroline Foxx

Diaper Rash

Treating Diaper Rash

Diaper rash can have a number of different causes: food allergies, reaction to chemicals in disposable diapers, or wet diapers, to name just a few.

If you recently started your baby on a solid food or different formula, limit your use of it for a few days to see if the rash lessens.

- The earlier a rash is treated, the more quickly it will respond.

- Change diapers more frequently than normal. Keep baby dry.

- Gently rinse or wash the diaper area with lukewarm water and mild soap, especially after bowel movements.

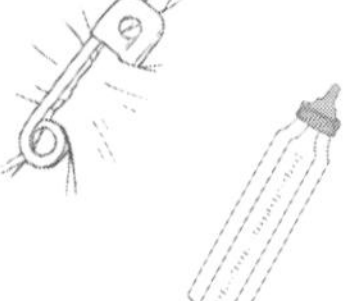

Cradle cap looks like crusty scaly areas around the scalp and eyebrows. To remove, rub affected areas with a little baby oil. Let soak in, then scrub off during bathtime.

Susy Stone

Bath Time

- The bathing room should be warm.
- The bath water should be approximately at body temperature.
- All necessary supplies for the bath, and for later dressing, should be within easy reach. The newborn should never be left alone in the bath or on the changing table!
- A wet baby is slippery and requires both hands of the parent.

The Well Baby Book

We made the determination early on not to take "naked baby pictures." Bath time photos showed our boys in swimsuits. Today, as adults, they are grateful to me for that respect.

Anna Hawkins

If you feel nervous at first for fear you'll drop the baby in the water, you can soap her while she is on your lap or on a table. Then rinse her off in the tub, holding her securely with both hands.

Dr. Benjamin Spock

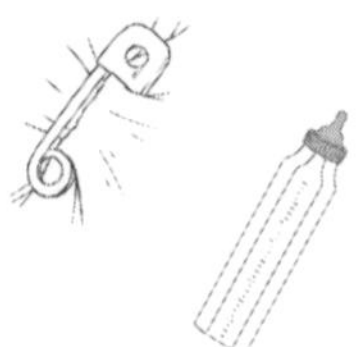

Symptoms of Teething

- Irritability
- Drooling
- Rubbing gums
- Chewing on objects
- Fretful sleeping

The best treatment for teething is to let the baby chew on smooth, firm, unbreakable objects. Teething rings are available in almost all stores and can be popped into the fridge to chill.

Newborns lose heat very quickly and need to be bundled up except in very warm temperatures.

The Well Baby Book

A man can be a warm father
and a real man at
the same time.

Dr. Benjamin Spock

Chapter 4

Dad's Eye View

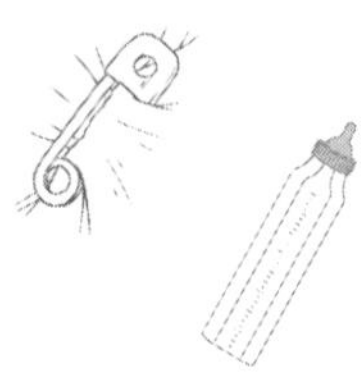

In today's world fathers are taking a more active role in the birth and rearing of the children. Gone are the days of fathers' waiting rooms, filled with nervous-pacing dads itching to hear the news before rushing to the pay phone to call relatives and friends. Yet so much attention is paid to new mothers and newborns that dad's feelings are often swept under the rug. Read on to find out more about the father's adjustments to a new baby in the home.

Sometimes I wonder why the good Lord gave the job of having children to women, when men could organize the process and turn them out in triplicate in half the time.

Erma Bombeck

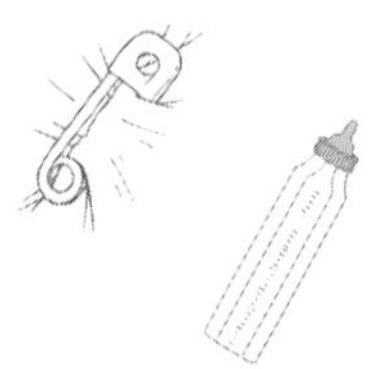

I remember leaning against, then sliding down, the wall in the room where my wife was in labor with our firstborn. After 10 hours of helping implement various Lamaze breathing/focusing techniques that we had learned together, after 30 hours of no sleep (what day and time is it?), with an energy-sapping sunburn from playing golf the previous afternoon that screamed louder than any new baby on the wing, I was near exhaustion.

It's a good thing we can't see into the future. As shoddy as I felt, there were *still* eight more hours of labor ahead before my wife would yield the precious object of our collective endeavor — Daren.

From the moment of delivery on, for the next 48 hours, I was on the highest high of my life. Sunburn, sleep deprivation — all vanished before the miracle of birth.

Alan Ross

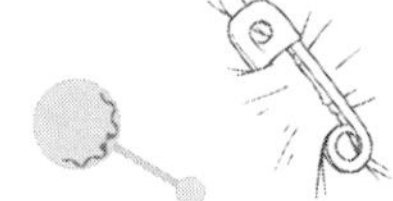

I would say that the surest measure of a man's or a woman's maturity is the harmony, style, joy, and dignity he creates in his marriage, and the pleasure and inspiration he provides for his spouse.

Dr. Benjamin Spock

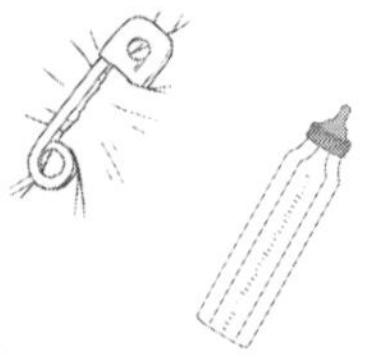

Advice for new dads

Sure, men don't get physically pregnant, but many dads-to-be experience the emotional roller coaster of pregnancy, with some even developing curious physical symptoms ~ feeling exhilaration and joy as well as fears, worries and anxieties about pregnancy and parenthood. These concerns are normal, but unfortunately they're often overlooked.

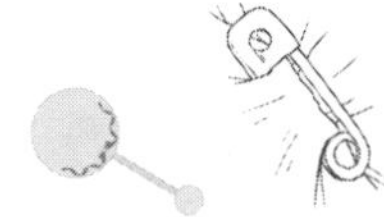

- A generation ago, a father-to-be was expected to do little more than bring home the paycheck and show up at the hospital with a box of cigars. Today, many men serve as labor coaches and are actively involved in their partners' pregnancies. While they may welcome these opportunities, some men struggle with the role. Are they one of the co-stars or part of the supporting cast? Without role models, they may be confused about how they're supposed to act and feel.

- Other fears involve life changes. During pregnancy, a man may grow apprehensive at the increased responsibilities ahead of him. Will he be a good father? Can he make enough money to provide for his family? Will he continue to be able to travel, see friends and have social activities after his child is born?

eshop.msn.com

It was Joseph who received into his arms the new-born Saviour; it was he who watched over His infancy, with more than the affectionate solicitude of a parent; it was he who laboured with his own hands for His subsistence.

St. Teresa

The more positive the mother's relationship with the father, the better the baby's fetal environment will be. In this way the father's role in pregnancy goes far beyond contributing half the baby's genetic constituents. His actions and attitudes have a direct effect on the mother and the fetal environment.

The Well Baby Book

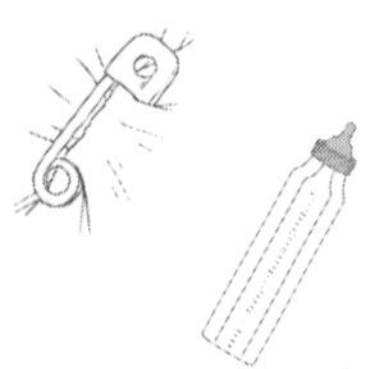

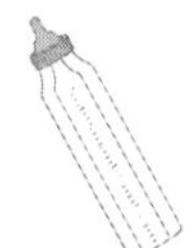

What a contribution a father makes when, realizing how limited his own world is, he seeks some new world for his own children.

Carlyle Marney

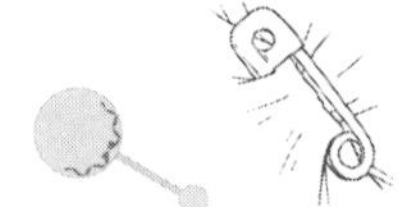

Perhaps the greatest social service that can be rendered by anybody to the country and to mankind is to bring up a family.

George Bernard Shaw

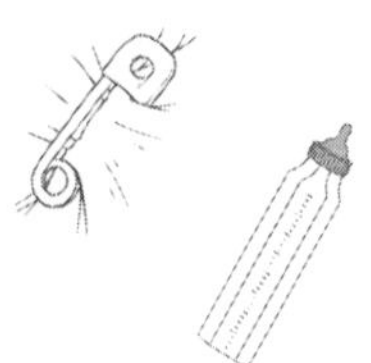

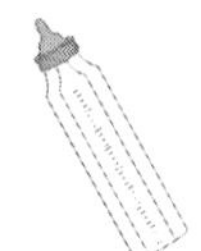

How to Tell You're a New Dad

- Getting six hours of sleep is a privilege.
- You are used to doing everything one-handed.
- The list of bodily fluids that disgust you has shortened, possibly to zero.
- Your idea of romance is holding hands.

- You answer the question "How are you?" with "We're fine."

- You decide whether a shirt is wearable not based on sweatiness, but based on how well the spit-up stains match the shirt's main color.

And the #1 way to tell that you're a new dad:

- You pass a car dealership and think, "Hey, nice van."

Evan Morton

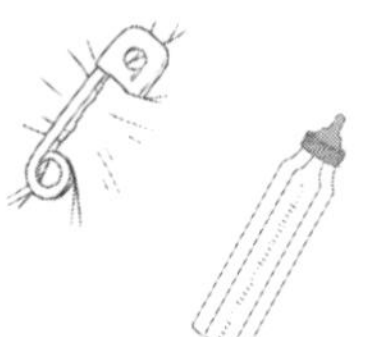

My Father is the one from whom I get my strength.

Jesus

Fathers must practice the business of letting the day slip off behind them as they come in the front door.

Carlyle Marney

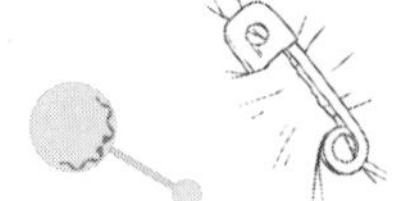

Marius: Who is the father, the one who gives life or the one who buys the bibs?

César: The Father is the one who loves!

Alphonse Daudet
from Sapho, *1884*

Wynken, Blynken, and Nod one night
Sailed off in a wooden shoe —
Sailed on a river of crystal light
Into a sea of dew....

Eugene Field

Chapter 5

Good Night, Moon (Goodbye Sleep)

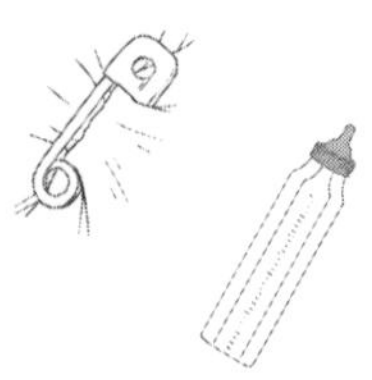

Put the baby to bed at a reasonable hour, say "good night" affectionately but firmly, walk out of the room, and don't go back.

Dr. Benjamin Spock

There never was a child so lovely but his mother was glad to get him asleep.

Ralph Waldo Emerson

Keep bedtime agreeable and happy. Remember that it is delicious and inviting to tired children if you don't turn it into an unpleasant duty. Expect them to turn in at the hour you decide as surely as you expect them to breathe.

Dr. Benjamin Spock

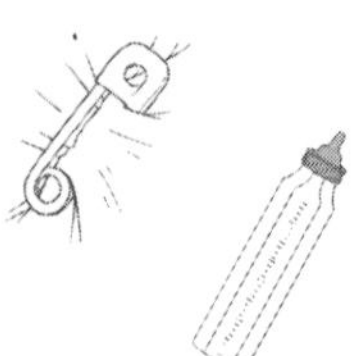

No animal is so inexhaustible as an excited infant.

Amy Leslie

How New Parents Can Avoid Fatigue

Most new parents experience considerable fatigue in the first few weeks due to extra work, extra company, stress and lack of sleep. In general, the more the baby wakes at night, the more tired the parents are. Here are helpful suggestions to make life easier:

- Take naps during the day as soon as the baby goes down for a nap.
- Go to sleep very early at night.
- Reduce or eliminate visitors ~ especially the ones who are stressful ~ limit their stay, set the time and length of the stay in advance.
- Make a conscious effort to rest; stay in bed; undertake nothing extra; simplify all household routines, especially meals, cleanup and baby laundry.
- Be alert to early signs of fatigue.
- Make use of relaxation, exercise, meditation, and imagery.

The Well Baby Book

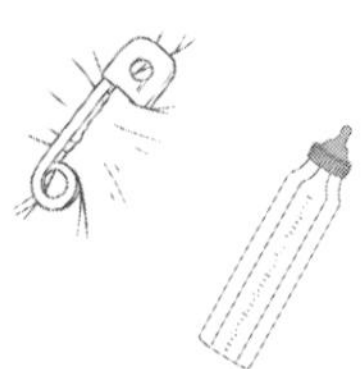

By the time the baby is three or
four months old its sleep patterns
are becoming more defined.

Mike Samuels, M.D.
Nancy Samuels

There was a place in childhood that
I remember well,
And there a voice of sweetest tone bright
fairy tales did tell.
My Mother dear.

Samuel Lover

People who say they
sleep like a baby
usually don't have one.

Leo Burke

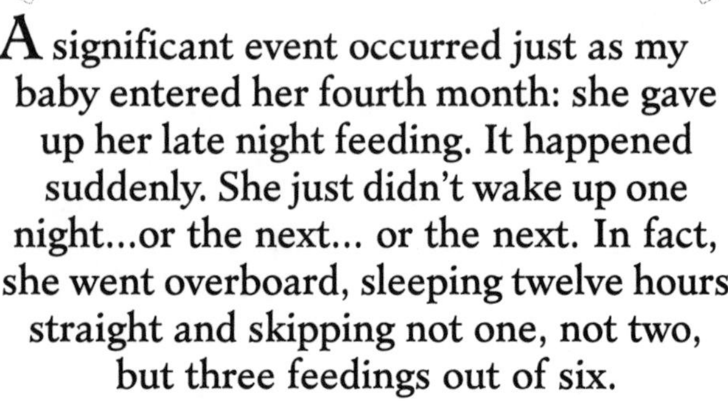
A significant event occurred just as my baby entered her fourth month: she gave up her late night feeding. It happened suddenly. She just didn't wake up one night...or the next... or the next. In fact, she went overboard, sleeping twelve hours straight and skipping not one, not two, but three feedings out of six.

Ann Kishbaugh

If you are not getting enough sleep, try napping during the day or early evening, or going to bed early at night. And recognize that, exhausting as this part of child care can be, wakefulness will decrease as your baby gets older. Eventually, you will get a full night's sleep again.

Robin Goldstein

Goodnight, Moon.
Goodnight, Room.
Goodnight, House.
Goodnight, Mouse.
Goodnight, Little Old Lady
Saying "Hush."
Goodnight, Ozzie.
Goodnight, Ricky.
Goodnight, John Boy.
(Go to sleep, Baby)

We American pioneers of the pacifier have given it the respectability it deserves. After all, what other force in the world has the power to heal, stop tears, end suffering, sustain life, restore world peace, and is the elixir that grants mothers everywhere the opportunity to sleep...perchance to dream?

Erma Bombeck

Chapter 6

Woobies

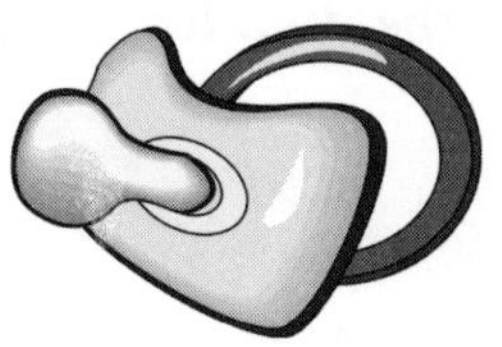

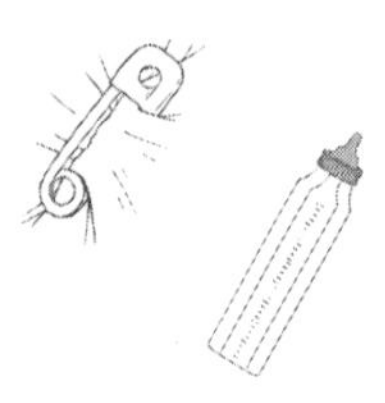

CAUTION: *DO NOT BE FOOLED BY THE NAME OF THIS CHAPTER!*

A woobie is not a laughing matter ~ regardless of what you call it.

A woobie is a pacy, foo-foo, binky, blankee, lovey, punny, ya-ya, moshie ~ the names are endless. If your baby has attached him/herself to a Woobie, be prepared to experience the dreaded woobie search.

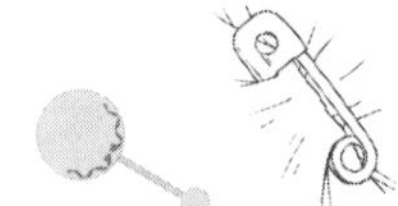

"I wost my woobie."

Call the detectives. Give them the clues that the item cannot be replaced and always disappears at night, at bedtime, when you and your kids are tired. Prepare to stop life as you know it until the missing item is found.

realmoms.com

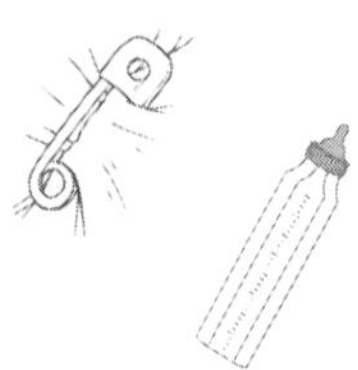

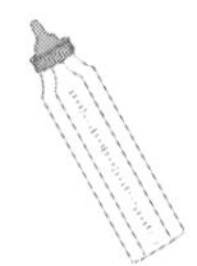

I conducted an experiment one night and found to my delight that a pacifier recovered from a package of coffee grounds in the garbage can be rinsed well under hot water and jammed quickly into baby's mouth, actually enjoying improved flavor.

Erma Bombeck

I was a closet pacifier advocate. So were most of my friends. Unknown to our mothers, we owned thirty or forty of those little suckers that were placed strategically around the house so a cry could be silenced in less than thirty seconds.

Erma Bombeck

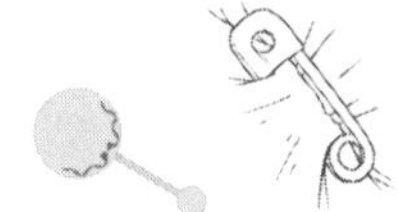

Some babies seem to have a need to suck that goes beyond their need for nourishment. Pacifiers are one way to meet this need. Such babies may happily suck on a pacifier for long periods of time, and this activity seems to soothe them.

Mike Samuels, M.D.
Nancy Samuels

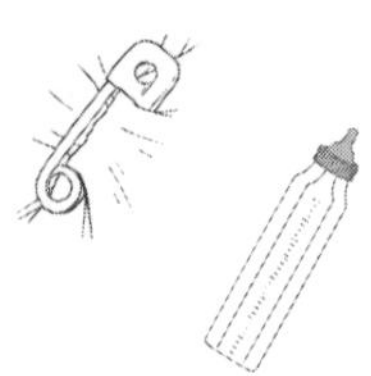

My mummy is my woobie.

Leslie Prince

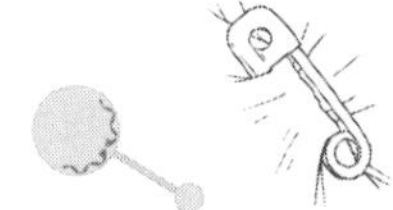

In discussing the ten most significant contributions to the quality of our lives, I don't care what women say, the number-one choice for me is the pacifier. How many women would be with us today were it not for that little rubber-plastic nipple that you jam in a baby's face to keep him from crying?

Erma Bombeck

Before I got married, I had six theories about bringing up children. Now I have six children and no theories.

John Wilmot

Chapter 7

Keep Smiling

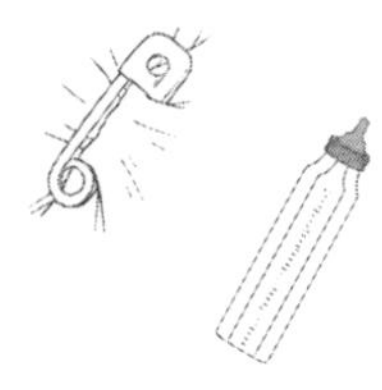

Parents are the bones on which children cut their teeth.

Peter Ustinov

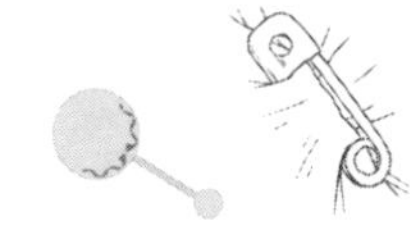

Giving birth is like taking your lower lip and forcing it over your head.

Carol Burnett

The phrase "working mother" is redundant.

Jane Sellman

Having a child is surely the most beautifully irrational act that two people in love can commit.

Bill Cosby

Think of stretch marks as pregnancy service stripes.

Joyce Armor

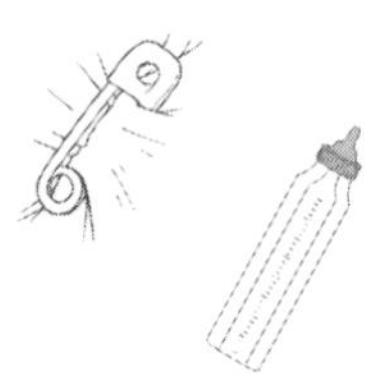

If evolution really works, how come mothers only have two hands?

Milton Berle

Cleaning your house while your kids are still growing is like shoveling the walk before it stops snowing.

Phyllis Diller

Having a family is like having a bowling alley installed in your brain.

Martin Mull

I don't know why they say,
"you have a baby."
The baby has *you*.

Gallagher

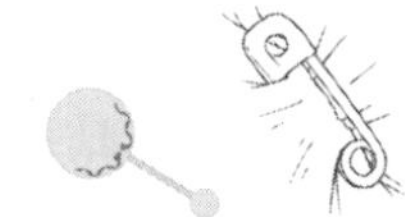

It is not economical to go to bed early to save the candles if the result is twins.

Chinese Proverb

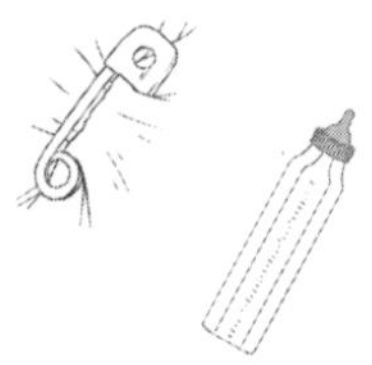

Raising kids is part joy and
part guerilla warfare.

Ed Asner

First you have to teach a child to talk,
then you have to teach him to be quiet.

Prochnow

A truly appreciative child will break,
lose, spoil, or fondle to death
any really successful gift within
a matter of minutes.

Russell Lynes

When I was born, I was so surprised
I couldn't talk for a year and a half.

Gracie Allen

Any child can tell you that the sole purpose of a middle name is so he can tell when he's in trouble.

Dennis Fakes

Even when freshly washed and relieved of all obvious confections, children tend to be sticky.

Fran Lebowitz

Children are supposed to help hold a marriage together. They do this in a number of ways. For instance, they demand so much attention that a husband and wife, concentrating on their children, fail to notice each other's faults.

Richard Armour

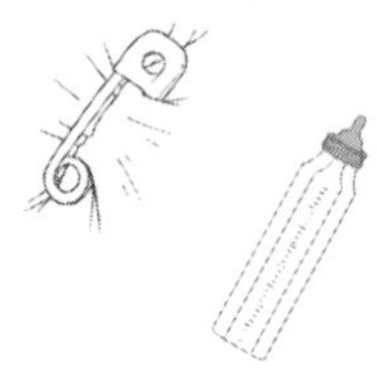

If your baby is "beautiful and perfect, never cries or fusses, sleeps on schedule and burps on demand, an angel all the time," you're the grandma.

Theresa Bloomingdale

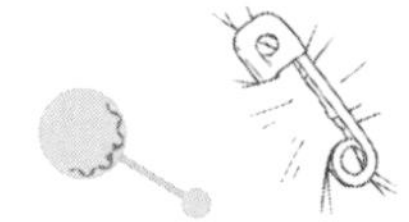

You can learn many things from children.
How much patience you have,
for instance.

Franklin P. Jones

Always be nice to your children because
they are the ones who will choose
your rest home.

Phyllis Diller

Everyone is in awe of the lion tamer in
a cage with half a dozen lions —
everyone, but a school bus driver.

Unknown

Pretty much all the honest truth-telling
in the world is done by children.

Oliver Wendell Holmes

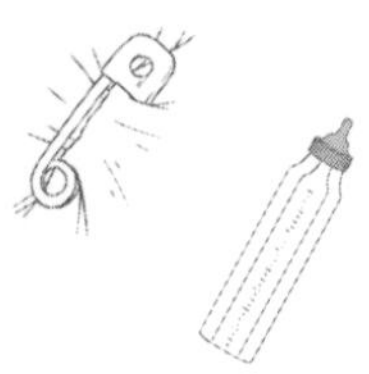

Invest in the future; have a child and teach her well.

Anonymous

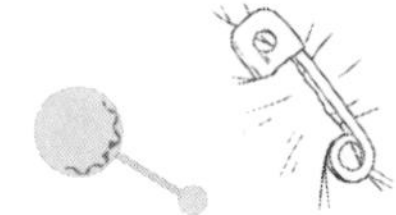

Laughter is like changing a baby's diaper. It doesn't permanently solve any problems, but it makes things more acceptable for a while.

Unknown

Don't tell me about the labor pains; show me the baby!

Jeanne Robertson

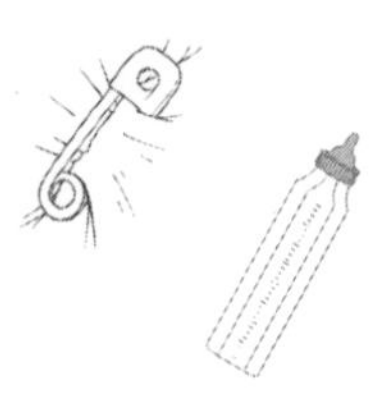

Families with babies and families without are so sorry for each other.

Ed Howe

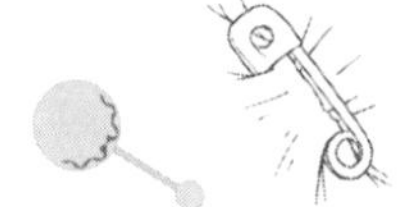

The best way to keep children at home is to make the home atmosphere pleasant — and let the air out of their tires.

Dorothy Parker

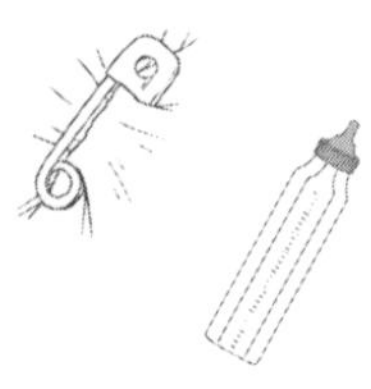

Human beings are the only creatures on Earth that allow their children to come back home.

Bill Cosby

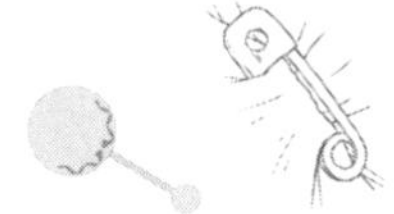

A father is always making his baby into a little woman. And when she is a woman he turns her back again.

Enid Bagnold

If you want a baby, have a new one. Don't baby the old one.

Jessamyn West

A three-year-old child is a being who gets almost as much fun out of a fifty-six dollar set of swings as it does out of finding a small green worm.

Bill Vaughan

I have found the best way to give advice to your children is to find out what they want and then advise them to do it.

Harry S. Truman

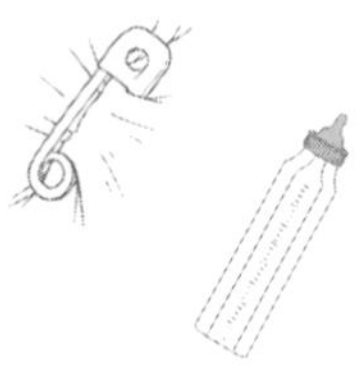

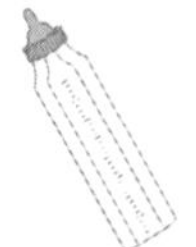

The thing that impresses me most about America is the way parents obey their children.

Edward, Duke of Windsor

Motherhood is an essential, difficult, and full-time job. Women who do not wish to be mothers should not have babies.

Edward Abbey

Advice to expectant mothers: you must remember that when you are pregnant, you are eating for two. But you must also remember that the other one of you is about the size of a golf ball, so let's not go overboard with it. I mean, a lot of pregnant women eat as though the other person they're eating for is Orson Welles.

Dave Barry

Here we have a baby. It is composed of a bald head and a pair of lungs.

Eugene Field

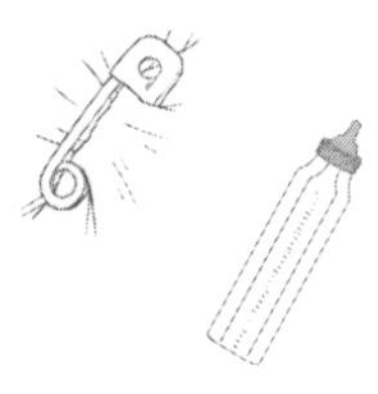

After having my first baby, I was overwhelmed with a feeling of privilege. I could not believe that on a planet with seven expansive continents, seventeen massive oceans and seas, and more than five billion people, this fragile individual had been entrusted to me.

Lori Borgman

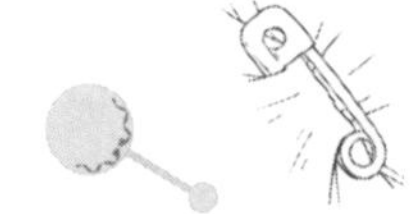

People often ask me,
"What's the difference between
couplehood and babyhood?"

In a word? Moisture.

Everything in my life is now
more moist. Between your
spittle, your diapers, your
spit-up and drool, you got your
baby food, your wipes, your
formula, your leaky bottles,
sweaty baby backs, and
numerous other
untraceable sources —
all creating an ever-present
moistness in my life, which
heretofore was mainly dry.

Paul Reiser
Babyhood

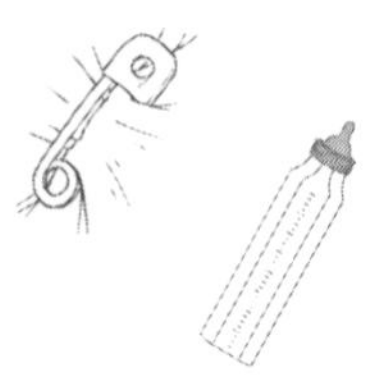

Almost everything a mother feels and almost everything a baby does is normal — even if it's not what the baby next door is doing.

Heidi E. Murkoft

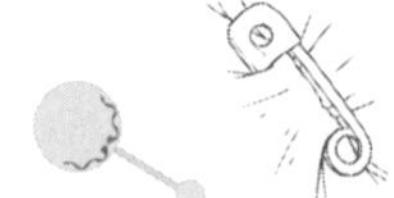

No matter what your child's rate of development, what is accomplished in the first year is remarkable — never again will so much be learned so quickly.

Sandee E. Hathaway

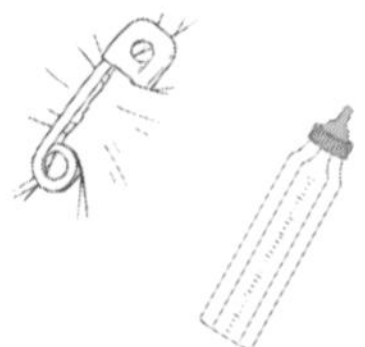

What's with these women who waddle into the hospital complaining of a bad case of indigestion and deliver twins two hours later? When presented with their case of indigestion swathed in pink blankets, they express shock and say, "I didn't even know I was pregnant!" I'm the suspicious type. I think when they got to the stage where they couldn't see their feet over their stomachs, couldn't fit behind a car steering wheel, couldn't wear anything but a tent with a drawstring neckline, they suspected, all right.

Erma Bombeck

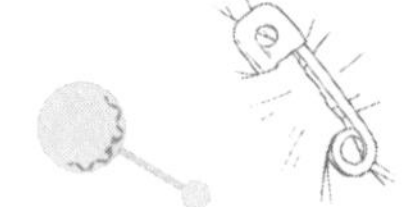

You are going to run out of answers by the time your child reaches the age of two, better known as "The Inquisition." You will swear your little one is in training to be a reporter. "How" and "Why" become the building blocks of every conversation and your answer will begin to form a life-long perception.

Motherwords

When people say: "Oh, doesn't Terry speak yet?" look them straight in the eye and answer: "We don't encourage him to speak. We hear that can really backfire on you."

Motherwords

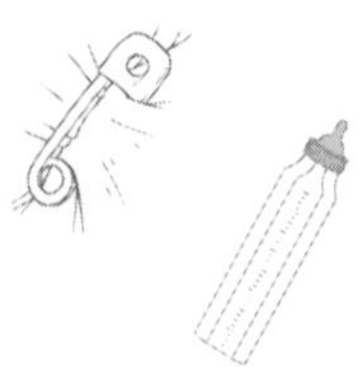

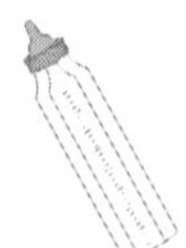

How hard could it be to care for a little baby that has the muscle tone of raw egg whites, doesn't eat real food, and spends most of the time sleeping?

Lori Borgman

You know your children are growing up when they stop asking you where they came from and refuse to tell you where they're going.

P.J. O'Rourke

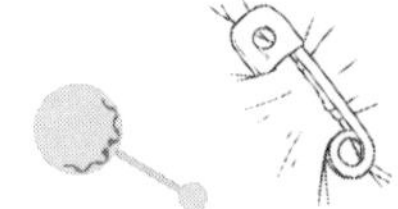

When your children are fighting one another in a public place, state firmly, "You just wait until I get you home to your mother!"

Motherwords

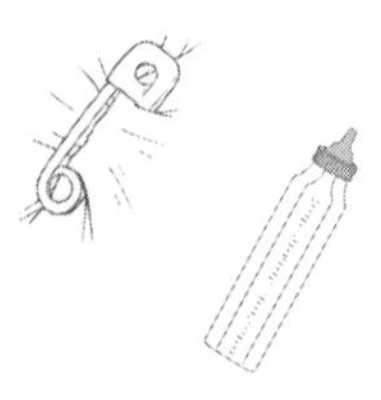

Friends and coworkers gave us three baby showers before our first child was born. I had everything imaginable a young wife would need to become a mother. I was prepared. Well prepared. I honestly believed that I would go to the hospital, push out a brand-new baby, and instantly become a mother.

Lori Borgman

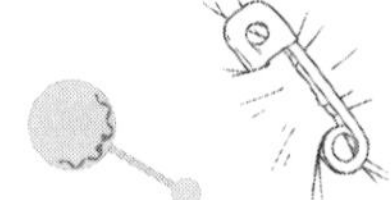

Why'd we have all these kids?

Jimmy Stewart
It's A Wonderful Life

Bibliography

Bibliography

Bombeck, Erma. Motherhood, The Second Oldest Profession. New York: McGraw-Hill, 1983.

Bombeck, Erma. The Best of Bombeck. New York City: Galahad Books, 1987.

Borgman, Lori. I Was A Better Mother Before I Had Kids. New York: Pocket Books, 1999.

Eisenberg, Arlene. What to Expect the First Year. New York: Workman, 1989.

Goldstein, Robin. Everyday Parenting. New York: Penguin Books, 1990.

Kisbaugh, Ann and Nevin. Bringing Up Baby. Chicago: Bonus Books, Inc., 1991.

Marney, Carlyle. Dangerous Fathers, Problem Mothers, and Terrible Twos. Nashville: Abingdon Press, 1958.

Maurer, Daphne and Charles Maurer. The World of the Newborn. New York: Basic Books, Inc., 1988.

Ribble, Margaret A. M.D. The Rights of Infants: Early Psychological Needs and Their Satisfaction. New York: Columbia University Press, 1943.

Samuels, Mike, M.D. and Nancy Samuels. The Well Baby Book. New York: Summit Books, 1996.

Spock, Dr. Benjamin. Baby and Child Care. New York: Hawthorn Books, 1946, 1976.

Spock, Dr. Benjamin. Raising Children in a Difficult Time. New York: W.W. Norton & Company, Inc., 1974.

Stephenson, Rev. W. S.J. Prayers to St. Joseph. Dublin, Ireland: Office of the "Irish Messenger," 1929.

Wiener, Joan and Joyce Glick. Adventures in Pregnancy, Birth and Being a Mother. New York: Collier Books, 1974.

Wolfe, Marty Burns and Foyne Mahaffey and Laura Manthey. In Motherwords. New York: Carroll & Graf Publishers, Inc., 1996.

When your child says,
"Do I have to?"
don't even answer.

In Motherwords

Index

A

B

C

D

E

F

G

H

I

J

K

L

M

O

P

R

S

T

U

V

W

Best thing you can do
for you kids?
Just love 'em.

John Cooper

About the Author

Karol Cooper lives with her husband, Alan Ross, in Monteagle, Tennessee. She is the author of three books by Walnut Grove Press. Karol writes for *Country Rag*, an internationally award-winning magazine presenting Appalachia folklore and artists, and is a freelance editor and typesetter.

She is the proud mother of three sons: Benjamin, Jake and Zach, and an avid gardener.

Other Books by Karol Cooper

Love is Forever (cowritten with Alan Ross)
Mothers and Daughters Forever